I0482952

Lean IT: Key to Improvement of Carbon Footprints

By Ade Asefeso MCIPS MBA

Second Edition

ISBN-13: 978-1499774283

ISBN-10: 1499774281

Publisher: AA Global Sourcing Ltd
Website: http://www.aaglobalsourcing.com

Table of Contents

Disclaimer...5

Dedication...6

Chapter 1: Introduction 7

Chapter 2: Lean in IT 11

Chapter 3: Lean IT Principles 15

Chapter 4: Simple Rules for Achieving Lean IT ...19

Chapter 5: Waste in IT.............................23

Chapter 6: Visual Management Systems for IT 25

Chapter 7: Challenges for Lean IT.............31

Chapter 8: Trends Towards Lean IT 35

Chapter 9: Factory and Enabling IT 39

Chapter 10: Deployment and Commercial Support
....51

Chapter 11: Reducing Application Maintenance
Costs..53

Chapter 12: Conclusion.............................57

Disclaimer

This publication is designed to provide competent and reliable information regarding the subject matter covered. However, it is sold with the understanding that the author and publisher are not engaged in rendering professional advice. The authors and publishers specifically disclaim any liability that is incurred from the use or application of contents of this book.

Dedication

This book is dedicated to the hundreds of thousands of incredible Head Teachers and Teachers in the world who have weathered through the up and down of inspiring us and making us what we are today.

This book is dedicated to my lovely boys, Thomas, Michael and Karl. Teaching them to manage their finance will give them the lives they deserve. They have taught me more about life, presence, and energy management than anything I have done in my life.

Chapter 1: Introduction

Lean IT is the extension of lean manufacturing and lean services principles to the development and management of information technology (IT) products and services. Its central concern, applied in the context of IT, is the elimination of waste, where waste is work that adds no value to a product or service.

Although lean principles are generally well established and have broad applicability, their extension from manufacturing to IT is only just emerging. Indeed, Lean IT poses significant challenges for practitioners while raising the promise of no less significant benefits. And whereas Lean IT initiatives can be limited in scope and deliver results quickly, implementing Lean IT is a continuing and long-term process that may take years before lean principles become intrinsic to an organization's culture.

Extension of Lean to IT

As lean manufacturing has become more widely implemented, the extension of lean principles is beginning to spread to IT (and other service industries). Industry analysts have identified many similarities or analogues between IT and manufacturing. For example, whereas the manufacturing function manufactures goods of value to customers, the IT function "manufactures" business services of value to the parent organization and its customers. Similar to manufacturing, the development of business services entails resource management, demand management, quality control, security issues, and so on.

Moreover, the migration by businesses across virtually every industry sector towards greater use of online or e-business services suggests a likely intensified interest in Lean IT as the IT function becomes intrinsic to businesses' primary activities of delivering value to their customers. Already, even today, IT's role in business is substantial, often providing services that enable customers to discover, order, pay, and receive support. IT also provides enhanced employee productivity through software and communications technologies and allows suppliers to collaborate, deliver, and receive payment.

Consultants and evangelists for Lean IT identify an abundance of waste across the business service "production line", including legacy infrastructure and fractured processes. By reducing waste through application of lean Enterprise IT Management (EITM) strategies, CIOs (Chief Information officers) and CTOs (Chief Technology officers) in companies such as Tesco, Fujitsu Services, and TransUnion are driving IT from the confines of a back-office support function to a central role in delivering customer value.

Types of Waste in Lean IT

Lean IT promises to identify and eradicate waste that otherwise contributes to poor customer service, lost business, higher than necessary business costs, and lost employee productivity. To these ends, Lean IT targets eight elements within IT operations that add no value to the finished product or service or to the parent organization.

Waste Element	Examples	Business Outcome
Defects	• Unauthorized system and application changes. • Substandard project execution.	Poor customer service, increased costs.
Overproduction (Over-provisioning)	• Unnecessary delivery of low-value applications and services.	Business and IT misalignment, Increased costs and overheads: energy, data center space, maintenance.
Waiting	• Slow application response times. • Manual service escalation procedures.	Lost revenue, poor customer service, and reduced productivity.
Non-Value Added Processing	• Reporting technology metrics to business managers.	Miscommunication.
Transportation	• On-site visits to resolve hardware and software issues. • Physical software, security and compliance audits.	Higher capital and operational expenses.
Inventory (Excess)	• Server sprawl, underutilized hardware. • Multiple repositories to handle risks and control. • Benched application development teams.	Increased costs: data center, energy; lost productivity.

Motion (Excess)	• Fire-fighting repeat problems within the IT infrastructure and applications.	Lost productivity.
Employee Knowledge (Unused)	• Failing to capture ideas/innovation • Knowledge and experience retention issues and employees spend time on repetitive or mundane tasks.	Talent leakage, low job satisfaction, increased support and maintenance costs.

Whereas each element in the table above can be a significant source of waste in itself, linkages between elements sometimes create a cascade of waste (the so-called domino effect). For example, a faulty load balancer (waste element: Defects) that increases web server response time may cause a lengthy wait for users of a web application (waste element: Waiting), resulting in excessive demand on the customer support call centre (waste element; Excess Motion) and, potentially, subsequent visits by account representatives to key customers' sites to quell concerns about the service availability (waste element; Transportation). In the meantime, the company's most likely responses to this problem; for example, introducing additional server capacity and/or redundant load balancing software), and hiring extra customer support agents may contribute yet more waste elements (Over-provisioning and Excess Inventory).

Chapter 2: Lean in IT

IT is the next frontier for the application of Lean in business. This powerful methodology has significant impact without being capital intensive.

IT has reached an unprecedented level of complexity, and organizations heavily reliant on IT risk greater variability in performance and significantly lower customer satisfaction. The Lean continuous-improvement methodology addresses these challenges. Lean methodology has been successfully deployed in IT operations having overcome two major hurdles: IT work is less repeatable and less directly observable or measurable than traditional engineering processes.

Hind Sight ICT application of Lean methodology takes an end-to-end view, starting with the IT customer. This ensures that improvement occurs across all IT processes. Hind Sight ICT approach has proven to have significant and lasting impact for end-users.

Hind Sight ICT had achieved very significant productivity improvements. In all cases, quality of service and employee satisfaction also improved significantly. For example, the average time to restore services has fallen by 50–80 percent, and quality compliance has risen by 5–10 percent.

By applying Lean principals to application maintenance and development Hind Sight ICT have helped clients to improve productivity by 15–25 percent, and time-to-market has fallen by up to 25 percent.

Hind Sight ICT help clients drive higher quality and productivity by taking IT infrastructure, application development, and maintenance work practices and moving them toward a set of consistent standards that drive higher quality and productivity. Hind Sight ICT brings about real change by working closely with the frontline staff and management teams to capture and sustain this impact.

Hind Sight ICT focus on the four core elements of balanced performance improvement:

1. Operating practices

Hind Sight ICT use a proven set of levers to enhance the way physical assets and resources are configured and optimized to create value and minimize losses.

2. Management systems

Hind Sight ICT optimizes the structures, processes and systems through which performance is managed to deliver business objectives.

3. Mindsets and behaviours

Hind Sight ICT focus on how to change the way people think, feel and conduct themselves in the workplace.

4. Organization and capabilities

Hind Sight ICT ensures the organization enables and sustains the transformation and that individuals have the skills and knowledge to deliver on their responsibilities.

Chapter 3: Lean IT Principles

Value Streams

In IT, value streams are the services provided by the IT function to organization for use by both internal and external customers, suppliers, employees, investors, regulators, the media, and any other stakeholders. These services may be further differentiated into:

1. Business services (primary value streams) Examples: point-of-sale transaction processing, ecommerce, and supply chain optimization.

2. IT services (secondary value streams) Examples: application performance management, data backup, and service catalogue.

The distinction between primary and secondary value streams is meaningful. Given Lean IT's objective of reducing waste, where waste is work that adds no value to a product or service, IT services are secondary (i.e. subordinate or supportive) to business services. In this way, IT services are tributaries that feed and nourish the primary business service value streams. If an IT service is not contributing value to a business service, it is a source of waste. Such waste is typically exposed by value-stream mapping.

Value-Stream Mapping

Lean IT, like its lean manufacturing counterpart, involves a methodology of value-stream and analyzing services (value streams) into their component process steps and eliminating any steps (or even entire value streams) that don't deliver value.

Flow

Flow relates to one of the fundamental concepts of Lean as formulated within the Toyota Production System; namely, Mura. A Japanese word that translates as "unevenness," Mura is eliminated through just-in-time systems that are tightly integrated. For example, a server provisioning process may carry little or no inventory with labour and materials flowing smoothly into and through the value stream.

A focus on Mura reduction and flow may bring benefits that would be otherwise missed by focus on muda (the Japanese word for waste) alone. The former necessitates a system-wide approach whereas the latter may produce suboptimal results and unintended consequences. For example, a software development team may produce code in a language familiar to its members and which is optimal for the team (zero muda). But if that language lacks an API standard by which business partners may access the code, a focus on Mura will expose this otherwise hidden source of waste.

Pull/Demand System

Pull (also known as demand) systems are themselves closely related to the aforementioned flow concept. They contrast with push or supply systems. In a pull system, a pull is a service request. The initial request is from the customer or consumer of the product or service. For example, a customer initiates an online purchase. That initial request in turn triggers a subsequent request (for example, a query to a database to confirm product availability), which in turn triggers additional requests (input of the customer's credit card information, credit verification, processing of the order by the accounts department, issuance of a shipping request, replenishment through the supply-chain management system, and so on).

Push systems differ markedly. Unlike the "bottom-up," demand-driven, pull systems, they are "top-down," supply-driven systems whereby the supplier plans or estimates demand. Push systems typically accumulate large inventory stockpiles in anticipation of customer need. In IT, push systems often introduce waste through an over-abundance of "just-in-case" inventory, incorrect product or service configuration, version control problems, and incipient quality issues.

Chapter 4: Simple Rules for Achieving Lean IT

There is a tension between development and production that occurs across all businesses. For IT, it often means development versus operations. Managers that master "lean approaches" can learn to synchronize these two sides of the business.

The lean philosophy is intended to being the creative (development) and operations sides of the business together. The two sides are fundamentally different, and this has implications for developing initiatives. It's about certainty. On the operational excellence side, we are trying to find things that can be standardized and repeatable. On the development side, it's about leveraging uncertainty. If you talk to an agile person, and say; "Quality at the source, do it right the first time," they will look at you and say; "No, you have got to fail fast early and often. You have to learn from your mistakes, and settle on what works." On the development side, things need to be creative, unstructured and somewhat uncertain. On the production side, standardization is key and variation is to be avoided at all costs. So how do we bring these two sides together? By adopting lean principles, by working together, by learning together. There is learning in the production process, and there is certainly process in the creative process.

Below are our advice for moving to Lean IT

1. **Do not focus on costs:** Isn't that what everybody was focused on over the past four years? We can guarantee you can lose a pound of weight. If you want to lose a pound, you give a pound of blood. Losing weight by cutting costs in IT is very simple. Fire people, cut projects, reduce the service levels. Are we healthy? Are we bouncing back? Are we overburdened? Do we have the time for continuous improvement? Of course not.

2. **Build in "slack time":** One of the principle ways that a company like Toyota continually improves over time, and drives stability up is that every time employees are presented a problem, they are not only given the time, but they are required to stop the line. And not only fix whatever is wrong, but prevent it from happening again. Only by doing that can you improve over time, so that you have fewer interruptions, fewer line stops. Otherwise, people are too afraid to stop production for quality issues because they are afraid they will get into trouble for not meeting production quotas. If you plan slack for the day, that doesn't mean you wasted that time, we guarantee that time will be used constructively in some way. If you don't stop thinking that everybody being busy is a measure of success, then ... you are on the wrong road. But it's a very hard mental model to break.

3. **Develop people through continuous coaching and learning:** Develop people before you

develop software this takes a deliberate and sustained investment in time. And it will not happen on its own. It will be squeezed out by more urgent things, but not more important things.

4. **Know your value streams and who owns them:** The value streams owners are like orchestra conductors.

5. **Keep it simple:** Often, businesses will call in developers to write or deploy more software to solve a problem. However, one of the principles that get lost in the Agile Manifesto is when you talk to someone who truly gets the spirit of agile, the agile person will say: "No, I'm here to prevent more software from being written. I'm here to help you simplify your process. The agile mentality is to write less code, rather than to write more code faster."

6. **Make it visual:** The Kanban board, which provides a visual diagram of scheduling in a lean manufacturing environment, is a great tool for development and operations as well. In software teams, in IT operations, the moment they can put sticky notes, and visualize demand and work in process and problems and velocity, you have given them the ability to see where their problems. Until then it is just a jumble in their heads. It is up to us to help them see through that jumble.

7. **Think backward from customer value, not forward from IT capabilities:** Until you really know what is it like to be a customer of yourself, all you have in your head is a hypothesis. If you think you know what it means to be a customer, you need to experience that.

8. **Embrace uncertainty:** Somehow we come together, with a purpose as a team.

Chapter 5: Waste in IT

Cutting the fat and reducing waste are leading people to affixing "lean" to everything; lean manufacturing, lean process management and recently lean-IT.

Lean principles were originally applied to manufacturing processes and since IT is a process many of these practices apply.

Eliminating waste, what lean calls 'muda', is the essence of Lean thinking. Lean highlights seven sources of waste. How 'muda' applies to IT is the subject of this chapter.

1.   Overproduction – making things before they are needed is a source of waste. In IT overproduction comes when IT builds solutions or provides capacity that is in excess of the business requirements.

2.   Waiting – the time and resources consumed in between major steps in a process. In IT waiting happens in areas like user signoff, requirements definition, testing, and other areas. Waiting comes from multi-tasking that often comes from trying to fully-allocate IT resources.

3.   Transporting – the unnecessary movement and handling of work. This happens when you pass work between multiple teams, multiple companies and locations. A lack of clear process, poor coordination tools and weak management increase transporting in IT.

4.   Inappropriate Processing – involves resource overkill, also known as 'gold platting' solutions. Over-provisioning service levels, taking on extra requirements or building beyond business needs are IT examples of this form of waste.

5.   Unnecessary Inventory – in manufacturing the concern is Work-In-Progress (WIP). In IT the resources tied up working on multiple concurrent projects. Remember that active five projects means five investments and no results. Shorting cycle time and increasing throughput reduces the amount of WIP.

6.   Unnecessary / Excess Motion — refers to the unnatural acts that people are made to perform in doing their job. In IT excess motion can he thought of the 'hero' actions that are common in IT. Whenever you need a hero you are requiring excess motion.

7.   Defects – errors are the common focus of improvement disciplines like six-sigma. In IT defect removal concentrates on verification, validation and testing.

Every organisation should look at these sources of waste in their operations and work to eliminate them.

Chapter 6: Visual Management Systems for IT

Lean manufacturing advocates the use of visual management systems to present and share critical information and facilitate process efficiency. Examples of visual management systems include:

1. Status boards that show personnel availability.
2. Lights on machines showing status (red for unavailable, yellow for available and green for in use).
3. Performance metrics posted in public areas that show throughput and quality performance.

Perhaps the best-known is the kanban card system that production workers in the Toyota Production System use as inventory pull signals. These manually constructed visual management systems work well in discrete manufacturing industries like automotive and electronics because of the physically tangible nature of the work-in-process (WIP), and because the process steps being managed are typically conducted in a single location, on the manufacturing floor.

In IT, business services consist of bits and packets coursing through electronic infrastructure, the ultimate in intangible WIP. It's not visibly apparent which servers and infrastructure components are supporting which services. Moreover, the infrastructure and personnel supporting service offerings are often distributed across the globe. Here, then the need to visualize end-to-end transactions and the underpinning infrastructure of said transactions is even more critical. How can IT operations be streamlined, virtualized, automated or managed without visibility into what is going on in the IT environment? The answer is that IT managers need enterprise IT management systems that provide visual management of business and IT services. These systems require an understanding of the infrastructure and staff supporting services, insight into the performance and utilization of staff and assets, and most importantly a level of data consolidation and presentation.

To optimize critical business services and achieve Lean IT, there are four dimensions that need to be considered:
1. Transaction Visibility
2. Business-IT Engagement
3. Operational Excellence
4. Security and Compliance

1. Transaction Visibility

To improve customer value, it is important to know what the customer is experiencing in their business interactions. Are your critical business services supporting a reputation for first-class service and responsiveness or causing frustrated customers to seek out the competition?

Given that virtually all externally facing applications are web-based, it is incumbent that the performance of these critical systems be managed. Modern application performance management systems can both monitor the end-to-end customer experience to measure responsiveness and also quickly locate the root cause to avoid the finger-pointing engendered by manual and after-the-fact sleuthing into performance problems.

2. Business-IT Engagement

The economic downturn has not diminished the demands on IT. Business executives still require new or updated IT applications and services to support their strategic initiatives. Employees still need access to services and service support. Change requests are unabated and need to be prioritized, approved, scheduled and managed through a controlled process.

Meeting and shaping these demands requires that IT and business leadership engage in a governance process that uses business-focused metrics as decision support. Further, business users should be able to directly request (i.e., "pull") tactical and operational requests about the systems they use. Medium to large IT shops can only meet these requirements with modern project and portfolio management and service lifecycle management systems. Together, these systems can provide complete transparency into the cost, quality and function of every project and service so that the service portfolio can continuously be optimized.

IT has the ability to understand how systems are being used to execute business processes. This data can be brought to the business and waste can be discussed, decisions made, and action taken to improve the process and systems efficiency.

3. Operational Excellence

Strategies to achieve operational excellence include identifying and remediating bottlenecks, automating processes to reduce wait-time and errors, and optimizing IT asset utilization through virtualization and consolidation efforts. Just-in-time resourcing needs to become a key discipline within IT.

High-impact transactions are typically supported by web-based front-ends and a variety of infrastructure components, often spanning mainframe and distributed platforms. The mainframe, it should be noted, is an extremely lean platform due to its energy efficiency and extreme reliability. For optimal efficiency, it's advisable to leverage an infrastructure management system that can accommodate complex, heterogeneous environments and can integrate processes across all layers of the operating stack from applications to servers, networks and databases.

Controlled change management processes are also critical for achieving operational excellence. Change management solutions help ensure that changes are scheduled to avoid a negative impact on the business, and reduce the risk of error and unplanned downtime.

4. Security and Compliance

When focusing on optimizing services to deliver more value and reduce costs, risk and compliance is a necessary consideration. Proving that only authorized users have access to sensitive information to support compliance initiatives continues to be a challenging and expensive endeavour that may become even more complex if new financial regulation compliance mandates are rolled out in the aftermath of the financial crisis.

Integrated Security and Compliance solutions help streamline and automate processes to remove waste from compliance processes and reduce the cost of assuring and validating compliance. At many companies, compliance processes are highly manual and redundant; many different groups use their own spreadsheets or other fragmented tool-sets, which can quickly become out of synch leading to further risk. Centralizing compliance information and standardizing processes and tool-sets, can reduce risk, remove redundancies and increase agility to respond as regulations change.

Survive and Thrive

Tough times end. Winners prepare to thrive in up-times even as they intelligently survive downturns. Lean IT provides a recipe for survival that simultaneously lays the groundwork for growth. Said another way, Lean IT is as much or more about thriving as it is about surviving.

Chapter 7: Challenges for Lean IT

Value-Stream Visualization

Unlike lean manufacturing, from which the principles and methods of Lean IT derive, Lean IT depends upon value streams that are digital and intangible rather than physical and tangible. This renders difficulty in the visualization of IT value streams and hence the application of Lean IT. Whereas practitioners of lean manufacturing can apply visual management systems such as the kanban cards used in the Toyota Production System, practitioners of Lean IT must use Enterprise IT Management tools to help visualize and analyze the more abstract context of IT value streams.

Reference Implementations

As an emerging area in IT management, Lean IT has relatively few reference implementations. Moreover, whereas much of the supporting theory and methodology is grounded in the more established field of lean manufacturing, adaptation of such theory and methodology to the digital service-oriented process of IT is likewise only just beginning. This lack makes implementation challenging, as evidenced by the problems experienced with the March 2008 opening of London Heathrow Airport's Terminal 5. British airports authority BAA and airline British Airways (BA), which has exclusive use of the new terminal, used process methodologies adapted from the motor industry to speed development and achieve cost savings in developing and integrating systems at the new terminal. However, the opening was marred by baggage handling backlogs, staff parking problems, and cancelled flights.

Resistance to Change

The recommendations of Lean IT initiatives are likely to demand organizational, operational, and/or behavioural changes that may meet with resistance from workers, managers, and even senior executives. Whether driven by a fear of job losses, a belief that existing work practices are superior, or some other concern, such changes may encounter resistance. For example, a Lean IT recommendation to introduce flexible staffing whereby application development and maintenance managers share personnel is often met with resistance by individual managers who may have relied on certain people for many years. Also, existing incentives and metrics may not align with the proposed staff sharing.

Fragmented IT Departments

Even though business services and the ensuing flow of information may span multiple departments, IT organizations are commonly structured in a series of operational or technology-centric silos, each with its own management tools and methods to address perhaps just one particular aspect of waste. Unfortunately, fragmented efforts at Lean IT contribute little benefit because they lack the integration necessary to manage cumulative waste across the value chain.

Integration of Lean Production and Lean Consumption

Related to the aforementioned issue of fragmented IT departments is the lack of integration across the entire supply chain, including not only all business partners but also consumers. To this end, Lean IT consultants have recently proposed so-called lean consumption of products and services as a complement to lean production. In this regard, the processes of provision and consumption are tightly integrated and streamlined to minimize total cost and waste and to create new sources of value.

Chapter 8: Trends Towards Lean IT

Recessionary Pressure to Reduce Costs

The onset of economic recession in December 2007 was marked by a decrease in individuals' willingness to pay for goods and services especially in face of uncertainty about their own economic futures. Meanwhile, tighter business and consumer credit, a steep decline in the housing market, higher indirect taxes, massive lay-offs (redundancy), and diminished returns in the money and bond markets have further limited demand for goods and services.

When an economy is strong, most business leaders focus on revenue growth. During periods of weakness, when demand for goods and services are curbed, the focus shifts to cost-cutting. In-keeping with this tendency, recessions initially provoke aggressive (and some panic-ridden) actions such as deep discounting, clearance sales of excess inventory, wage freezes, short-time working, and abandonment of former supplier relationships in favour of less costly supplies. Although such actions may be necessary and prudent, their impact may be short-lived. Lean IT can expect to gather support during economic downturns as business leaders seek initiatives that deliver more enduring value than is achievable through reactive and generalized cost-cutting.

Proliferation of Online Transactions

IT has traditionally been a mere support function of business, in common with other support functions such as shipping and accounting. More recently, however, companies have moved many mission-critical business functions to the Web. This migration is likely to accelerate still further as companies seek to leverage investments in service-oriented architectures, decrease costs, improve efficiency, and increase access to customers, partners, and employees.

The prevalence of web-based transactions is driving a convergence of IT and business. In other words, IT services are increasingly central to the mission of providing value to customers. Lean IT initiatives are accordingly becoming less of a peripheral interest and more of an interest that is intrinsic to the core business.

Green IT

Though not born of the same motivations, Lean IT initiatives are congruent with a broad movement towards conservation and waste reduction, often characterized as green policies and practices. Green IT is one part of this broad movement.

Waste reduction directly correlates with reduced energy consumption and carbon generation. Indeed, IBM asserts that IT and energy costs can account for up to 60% of an organization's capital expenditures and 75% of operational expenditures. In this way, identification and streamlining of IT value streams supports the measurement and improvement of carbon footprints and other green metrics. For instance, implementation of Lean IT initiatives is likely to save energy through adoption of virtualization technology and data centre consolidation.

Chapter 9: Factory and Enabling IT

Despite decades of increasingly intensive use of information across industries, IT has remained a black box for many executives. Too often, the link between spending and performance has been unclear, if not problematic. As a result, leaders felt that their only course of action was to hire a competent CIO Chief Information Officer), throw increasing amounts of money at IT, and hope for the best. The economic disruptions of recent years, however, have tightened budgets and placed a premium on action, forcing companies to rethink IT's fundamental role.

In most organizations, IT began as a support function, leading to a one-dimensional management approach. However, technology-enabled products, interactive communications, and an "always on" information environment have thrust IT to the forefront, with critical implications for business growth and customer engagement. In addition, established practices, such as lean-management techniques, have highlighted the value of IT in reducing waste and increasing productivity.

This deeper recognition of IT's potential has given rise to a new management model consisting of two categories; "Factory IT" and "Enabling IT." Factory IT encompasses the bulk of an organization's IT activities, applying lessons from the production floor scale, standardization, and simplification to drive efficiency, optimize delivery, and lower unit costs.

Enabling IT is focused on helping organizations respond more effectively to changing business needs and gain a competitive advantage by spurring innovation and growth.

This approach goes beyond simply relabeling functions to include broader leadership, governance, and organizational changes, and IT leaders will need very different skills to manage each model. Business leaders will have to engage with IT in new ways. For instance, while IT standardization and consolidation increase responsiveness, speed to market, and cost effectiveness, managers may have fewer options to customize solutions. Likewise, more transparency and better metrics may come at the expense of unrestricted choice for configuration and architecture. In return, business leaders would get a new type of IT partner to support innovation, with skills to deliver IT-enabled capabilities quickly that drive both top and bottom-line growth. But they will need to treat such IT staff as full members of their group, offering incentives and rewards for exceptional performance.

Factory IT: More efficient IT services

The core elements of the typical IT function have changed radically over the past decade, and this evolution has enabled the Factory model. Ten years ago, a company might have felt compelled to create its own software to manage the supply chain and other activities; today, many configurable products can meet those needs. Similarly, expensive, single-purpose servers and the dedicated support staff they require can be replaced by commodity servers, often managed from half a world away.

Moreover, these standardized platforms can now be coupled with mature processes for managing broad swaths of IT, including basic infrastructure and many of the business applications. Under this configuration, IT activities can be restructured and continually improved much as any other business process, using a combination of lean techniques, automation, and outsourcing or cloud computing to drive down costs and improve quality.

There are three key components of the Factory model

1. Industrialized IT applying traditional business-management techniques to IT

Standardization decreases the resources and specialized development needed to support IT, allowing organizations to apply proven management methods from large industrial settings to reduce IT costs. Lean-management techniques have evolved well beyond manufacturing and are applicable to the types of skilled services found in IT. A company can typically create 20 to 30 percent or more in additional IT capacity by streamlining processes, automating routine functions, and eliminating redundancy. Major sources of IT waste include unnecessary functionality (for example, gold-plated systems with extra, noncore functions), work flow bottlenecks caused by inadequate cross-training, and frequent rework from bugs or constantly changing requirements.

Companies can benefit significantly by replacing customized systems with highly standardized offerings (for example, a Web server or e-mail platform that includes common hardware, applications, and support levels) and service catalogues (essentially à la carte menus that specify the cost of each service). These improvements increase cost transparency and highlight clear opportunities for further efficiency while also giving individual business units the freedom to customize certain features and functions.

Organizations should also recognize that not all processes have equal value and should set service and support levels accordingly. For instance, one bank applied the same exacting levels of support and performance for its critical core banking applications to an in-house employee service portal. By increasing the service portal's allowable downtime to five days a year, from just five hours, the bank saved hundreds of thousands of dollars in hardware, software, and staff expense.

In our experience, these measures often double workforce productivity by redeploying or reducing staff. A standardized IT environment also allows companies to select from a wider array of vendors whose scale and skills can further reduce costs and improve delivery. In addition, by avoiding customized hardware and operating systems, companies can more readily take advantage of a technology cost curve that has been dropping by 4 to 5 percent annually.

2. Flexible IT factories building IT that's more responsive to changing business conditions

IT tends to operate on a very long-term investment cycle consisting of large, multiyear projects, extended outsourcing deals, and durable infrastructure assets. As the pace of business change accelerates and organizations respond to shifting market conditions or more frequent M&A, IT leaders are often constrained by these investments. IT departments are starting to adapt in two ways:

The cloud: Cloud computing offers access to information, processing, and storage through the network or an external service provider. This mode of delivery allows companies to purchase computer processing as a service, rather than making up-front investments in IT capacity and in-house support staff. The New York Times, for example, digitized and catalogued more than 100 years of archived articles for its Web site in a 24-hour period by using Amazon.com's cloud offering, avoiding the need to configure and operate a set of servers for a onetime effort.

Agile software development. IT programmers are flocking to approaches that emphasize the very fast, iterative development of systems through close interactions with users, allowing continual feedback and programming refinement. This agility can deliver new systems and capabilities in a matter of weeks or months instead of years. A frequent iteration cycle also keeps IT developers and business users in sync on requirements and priorities. Agile development may not be right for every project. However, since this approach is most effective when business needs are shifting, it is gaining favour among many IT departments.

Together, the cloud and agility can make the IT factory more nimble, with lower costs and faster delivery.

> 3. Holistic business cases - cutting complexity through improved planning

For most companies, IT complexity increases gradually, as systems slowly evolve beyond their initial purpose, or through acquisitions, when new, sometimes duplicative systems are built for individual business units. Performance suffers over time, as ineffective IT slows product introductions, hampers customer interactions, and often makes post-merger integration more difficult.

IT leaders recognize the adverse effects of complexity, but replacing these systems involves a substantial commitment of resources; hardware, new applications, and staff and vendor time. The economics are difficult to justify given the short time horizons of many tough-minded CFOs (Chief Finance Officers), particularly since tangible benefits are often realized only in the longer term.

To manage complexity, companies are starting to employ a more holistic business case model that goes beyond the traditional, IT centric versions. This model includes realistic, verifiable cost benefit analysis to assess the impact of new systems on the entire organization. Critically, such plans also require a road map for how future projects might build on the investment. At one company, for instance, the business case to deliver a unified view of all customer data showed how better information management could enable follow-on projects for marketing systems, enhancing cross-selling opportunities.

Implementing Factory IT

The benefits of these business cases are twofold. First, they ensure that the simplification of processes and systems is a starting point for new project investments. Second, better visibility can show how seemingly small IT projects can deliver a high return on investment by improving standardization and service levels across the entire business.

Enabling IT: Supporting innovation and delivering business value

As the market-facing complement to the Factory model, Enabling IT focuses on creating new sources of value. This emphasis on innovation requires three things; ready access to relevant information, a willingness to test and learn, and close collaboration. Enabling IT supports these activities by developing the processes and technologies to launch a new sales channel, design a tech-enabled product feature, or increase customer retention through online offerings.

Where Factory IT is housed centrally, Enabling IT's employees function as an IT SWAT team for new initiatives or business imperatives and are often closely integrated with or even embedded in business units. The performance of these employees is rated on metrics such as responsiveness and flexibility rather than on their ability to deliver low unit costs. Where Factory IT focuses on long-term projects and on-time delivery, Enabling IT is typified by rapid prototyping and iterative development. Our survey results show that companies deploy Enabling IT to support innovation and growth in three ways.

1. Turning raw data into insight

The increasing volume of data is taxing the ability of companies to track, filter, and analyze information and turn it into useful, actionable insights. Organizations that build effective information systems can take advantage of emerging opportunities and respond more quickly to unseen market changes. With the rise of electronic health records and prescription data, for example, pharmaceutical companies need systems to structure and mine this information for trends on patient compliance or drug efficacy.

Resolving these issues requires a cross-functional group of IT experts, statistical analysts, and business leaders. IT must develop new technical capabilities to manage the massive amount of information, and IT leaders will need to collaborate more closely with management teams to extract its full value.

2. Supporting rapid experimentation

Where lean manufacturing and Factory IT seek to avoid errors, Enabling IT's mind-set tolerates (and even encourages) the mistakes that result from experimentation and iteration as long as they happen quickly, the outcomes are measured, and the lessons are incorporated into the team's thinking. More companies are embracing rapid experimentation as a way to develop, refine, and upgrade their services or products. Capital One and Google, for example, have been at the forefront of this trend with their credit cards and online services, respectively. That wave is spreading to traditional players: P&G's Vocalpoint, a network of mothers, provides feedback on new product ideas. Similarly, a leading fast-food company is using IT systems and analytics at test sites to gauge the impact of new menu choices on store-level revenue, operations, and customer experience.

Such experimentation requires the right set of technical capabilities and a flexible IT environment. Managers must employ tools to define, build, test, and improve new products quickly, integrating feedback from both internal stakeholders and a set of users or customers. Responsive IT support is a vital component of this effort. By assembling a team to work hand in hand with the managers on these new business offerings, IT provides essential support to help build and modify business processes and systems rapidly.

3. Web 2.0 - fostering new interaction models

IT has historically focused on automating high-velocity transactions for enterprise resource planning (ERP), supply chains, and customer relationship management (CRM). That focus is now shifting to lightweight Web 2.0 tools to support the more diverse transactions and more complex interactions that shape, review, and inform innovation. Tools range in complexity from simple executive blogs to more robust portals where users can collaboratively access and analyze data sets.

Often, these newer forms of knowledge sharing require little additional investment, since the content is largely user generated and the tools rely mostly on existing applications and infrastructure. In fact, these tools usually augment existing transactional systems rather than replace them, thus increasing the value of IT investments while holding down costs. Since users often drive the development of these collaborative tools, strategies that complement users' work practices and styles are most effective. Although such an endeavour is challenging, the payoff can be substantial.

Enabling IT: Bringing it together

Innovation is seldom neat, and these collaborative systems are no exception. Successful initiatives usually start as small side projects or tests that gain critical mass rapidly, often with little regard for corporate technology or security standards. IT leaders can play a critical role by selecting and validating platforms, setting policies, and promoting capabilities to potential participants. Because Enabling IT staff members already work within business units, they can help guide these projects, giving executives some degree of control and assurance on compliance with critical security and data standards. The result is a smoother transition to the Factory IT environment when the systems reach maturity.

While leading companies may implement these principles differently based on their business needs and culture, we believe there is no turning back. Factory IT's potential to increase efficiency and reduce costs can finance the next wave of Enabling IT's innovation. The combination of functional productivity and business value creation will likely be a major competitive differentiator; the first step in delivering this value is to ensure companies have the right leaders in place for each effort.

Chapter 10: Deployment and Commercial Support

Deployment of Lean IT has been predominantly limited to application development and maintenance (ADM). This focus reflects the cost of ADM. Despite a trend towards increased ADM outsourcing to lower-wage economies, the cost of developing and maintaining applications can still consume more than half of the total IT budget. In this light, the potential of Lean IT to increase productivity by as much as 40% while improving the quality and speed of execution makes ADM a primary target (the "low-hanging fruit," so to speak) within the IT department.

Opportunity to apply Lean IT exists in multiple other areas of IT besides ADM. For example, service catalogue management is a Lean IT approach to provisioning IT services. When, say, a new employee joins a company, the employee's manager can log into a web-based catalogue and select the services needed. This particular employee may need a CAD workstation as well as standard office productivity software and limited access to the company's extranet.
On submitting this request, provisioning of all hardware and software requirements would then be automatic through a lean value stream.

In another example, a Lean IT approach to application performance monitoring would automatically detect performance issues at the customer experience level as well as trigger, notify support personnel, and collect data to assist in root-cause analysis. Research suggests that IT departments may achieve sizable returns from investing in these and other areas of the IT function.

Among notable corporate examples of Lean IT adopters is UK-based grocer Tesco, which has entered into strategic partnerships with many of its suppliers, including Procter & Gamble, Unilever, and Coca-Cola, eventually succeeding in replacing weekly shipments with continuous deliveries throughout the day. By moving to eliminate stock from either the back of the store or in high-bay storage, Tesco has gotten markedly closer to a just-in-time pull system.

Lean IT is also attracting public-sector interest, in-keeping with the waste-reduction aims of the Lean Government movement. One example is the City of Cape Coral, Florida, where several departments have deployed Lean IT. The city's police records department, for instance, reviewed its processing of some 20,000 traffic tickets written by police officers each year, halving the time for an officer to write a ticket and saving $2 million. Comparable benefits have been achieved in other departments such as public works, education, finance, fire, and parks and recreation.

Chapter 11: Reducing Application Maintenance Costs

Maintenance requirements can vary significantly. Peaks can occur because of spikes in transaction volumes or spikes in business enhancement/support requests caused by a lack of system flexibility. These spikes increase incidents and user support requirements.

Maintenance organizations "Hedge their bets" when it comes to maintenance. They deploy a fixed team of people who are pre-trained in the application so they can respond to high priority work quickly during these spikes. The size of the team is set to handle the spikes. As a result, they have excess capacity (and excess costs) when maintenance is not spiking.

Why does this happen?

1. Responding quickly to problems and high priority maintenance requires prior knowledge of the application. Development teams create specification documentation and user guides but they do not document the type of knowledge required to support and maintain applications. This knowledge is usually communicated by "word of mouth" over a long period of time so maintenance teams cannot rapidly adjust the available resources to respond to spikes.

2. Most incidents are the result of recurring problems. The support staff responds to the initial incident but

they rarely fix the underlying cause to permanently eliminate the problem so the recurring problems contribute to these spikes in support. This type of continuous improvement should occur when maintenance is not spiking.

3. Systems are designed and built to require maintenance because adding user controlled parameters and robust data validation increases the development costs. These decisions increase future maintenance costs and impact reliability.

How do we reduce spikes in maintenance and reduce the total cost?

1. Fix recurring problems to reduce maintenance spikes and total maintenance costs.

2. Add functionality to increase flexibility with user-controlled parameters to reduce the need for enhancements and user support.

3. Document support knowledge and cross-train others so that people can multi-task across applications to balance spikes in maintenance. This improves utilization of staff and allows staff to be shared across applications so that Application Maintenance staff costs are reduced.

Does this work? I have managed Application Maintenance outsourcing engagements for more than 20 years and we routinely delivered the same or better levels of support while reducing staffing levels/costs by 30-50% using these recommendations.

In addition to these recommendations, development teams must avoid adding long-term maintenance requirements when they build applications by including user-controlled parameters to enhance flexibility, ensure adequate data validation, and mandate planning/testing for processing spikes.

Chapter 12: Conclusion

Lean has been successfully applied to domains beyond manufacturing, including to enterprise IT on a case-by-case basis. The beauty of Lean is its pragmatism. It rewards and even encourages incremental wins, doesn't require a grand overhaul of systems, and isn't obscure in its methodology, terminology or theory.

IT Value Streams

The core philosophy of Lean can be summarized in four words: Maximize Value, Minimize waste. Lean focuses on analyzing and optimizing Value Streams (the sequence of activities to design, produce and deliver a good or service) to remove non-value added activity, or waste.

Value is always defined from the standpoint of the end customer. For IT, the end customers include the executives running the business and the users (employees, customer customers, and suppliers) of the services IT delivers. Thus, IT's Value Streams are the applications and/or services that IT delivers to and for the business, along with the care and feeding of these applications and services.

To make IT improvement projects understandable to the business and to maximize their positive impact on the business, IT should analyze infrastructure and processes from a vertically-integrated point of view. That is, rather than trying to horizontally improve data-centre operations supporting all business processes, a vertically-integrated approach would focus on optimizing infrastructure and processes supporting high-impact Value Streams first. These high impact Value Streams are often, but not always, "cash-register" applications in that they directly drive company revenue and are used primarily by external (paying) consumers. Examples include point-of-sale or eCommerce applications.

Waste Not

In a physical manufacturing plant, tell-tale signs of waste and bottlenecks, such as stockpiles of inventory or work-in-progress, are easily visible; not so in IT and yet, undoubtedly waste exists in even the best-run IT organizations. Server sprawl, underutilized hardware, manual processes, redundant applications, slows application response times. These are just a few of the signs of waste in IT.

Let the Value Flow

In Lean, the principle of Flow dictates that the value-added steps in a given process should flow in a tight and integrated sequence. As you remove waste from IT, it's critical to ensure that the remaining process steps are integrated to optimize service delivery. It is especially critical to consider the handoff points between different departments as these hand off points are often where wait-time is introduced.

Here, integrated management solutions can automate the workflow between different departments, minimizing wait-time. Management tools can further support optimizing flow by automating key process steps. The degree to which different departments use a set of integrated tools and processes helps optimize the flow of value to the customer.

An example of this is change management. Suppose a business unit wants to adapt a given customer-facing application to add in features that would differentiate the service from competitive offerings. Supporting this business project requires tight collaboration between the application development team that would make the code changes, the operations team that would need to assess the impact of these changes on other services, the Change Advisory Board that would review, approve and schedule the proposed changes, and the operations team that would deploy the updated application.

Just-in-Time IT

Another key Lean principle is Pull, which states that no step should occur until triggered by a "pull" signal from the downstream step. For instance, just as Dell didn't start building a computer till getting an order for it, IT shouldn't provision servers till they are needed. Compare this to the more traditional "push" control mechanism, where capacity or inventory is stockpiled in anticipation of need. While pushing capacity into inventory provides a buffer against urgent demand, more often than not it results in waste through incorrect configuration, version control problems, and incipient quality problems, not to mention the carrying cost of maintaining idle infrastructure.

Therefore, one of the primary goals of Lean improvement initiatives is to reduce cycle times to remove the need to perform operations in advance of their pull signals. For instance, if server provisioning takes days or weeks, there will be an inclination to have stand-by servers' provisioned just-in-case. A Lean approach would entail streamlining the provisioning process so that it takes only hours or minutes and resources can be provisioned just-in-time.

Along with cycle time reduction, significant attention must be paid to the form and mechanism of pull signals within IT Value Streams. For instance, pull signals from business executives may be handled through the portfolio planning mechanism of an IT Governance process, while initial pull signals from end users can be captured when they request a service via an actionable Service Catalogue system. Ongoing pull signals from users stem from real-time transaction volumes, which must be monitored and managed via application performance management coupled to scalable back-end provisioning.

Strive for Perfection

Another critical Lean principle is perfection, the Lean IT approach recognizes that great gains can be achieved through incremental improvement and that the journey to perfection never ends.

Keep improving!!

www.ingramcontent.com/pod-product-compliance
Lightning Source LLC
Chambersburg PA
CBHW071812170526
45167CB00003B/1276